T0368125

Reborn Among The Roses

Poems Along The Way

KENNETH E. GRANT

authorHOUSE·

AuthorHouse™
1663 Liberty Drive
Bloomington, IN 47403
www.authorhouse.com
Phone: 833-262-8899

Published by AuthorHouse 10/15/2024

ISBN: 979-8-8230-3549-1 (sc)
ISBN: 979-8-8230-3550-7 (hc)
ISBN: 979-8-8230-3548-4 (e)

Library of Congress Control Number: 2024921214

Print information available on the last page.

CONTENTS

Section III
Along the Way

Section IV
Nearing the Top... and Over

Final Thoughts

Dedicated to my dear son and our family

FOREWORD

The poems in this book might be called reflection of my later years, They reflect the variety of experiences life has offered and the many wonderful people I have been privileged to know. Each poem reflects the unique emotional impact these experiences have made on this admittedly sentimental soul.

Many thanks to scholar and friend Dr. Nancy Macky not only for her encouragement but also for her hours of careful reading and editing my three books of poetry.

WRITING POEMS

Writing poems is a chore
Although I'm glad to try and do it
To find a rhyme to fill the bill
I often have to say
I blew it

Resorting to another style
I often choose free verse
A simple sort of expression
Though making words echo
Now and then
Leads to this conclusion

Not every poem needs a rhyme
Or even meter
And sometimes I find
In fact
The resulting poem
Is better

Section I
The Natural World

A GARDEN WALK

I walked today in the garden
And paused
Amid the embrace
Of dewy moistened leaves
Surrounded by an
Abundance of blooms
Where bees searched
The hearts of flowers
My heart was already there
Raptured by a beauty
That bore the scent
Of holiness

The soft breeze
Though unseen
Breathed a quiet blessing
And bestowed
Upon my waiting heart
A gentle
Benediction

BEAUTIFUL MIND

In the mind
Where
Beauty may be found
Judgments made
From the eyes observing
The mind declares
Beautiful
Or not

Agreements
Coincide
Judgments gather
Values attach
Then the observed
Is declared
Beautiful
By agreeing minds

Earth is filled
With a thousand kinds
Of beauty
Seen
Then shared

When judgments
Coincide
Hearts and skillful hands
Agree
A thing of beauty
Born

Opening yet
Another door
For searching eyes
Listening ears
Open minds

Discovering beauty
In symphony
Or lilting tune
Lovely garden
A simple cottage
Or cathedral
Everywhere
Abundant
In this
Ever-changing
World

BEAUTY IN THE GRASS

Today I walk a path
Beside
A wide and well-kept lawn
Overshadowed by a tree
Whose leafy branches
Filter the sunlight
Creating patterns
Of light and shadow
On the grass
Then I pause
Wondering
If indeed
Patterns like this
Every life must show

Yet
There is hidden in the grass
Tiny blossoms blooming
Here and there
Petite snowy faces
White petal halos
Circling a drop of gold

Those who hurry by
May not see them
Hidden by the greening spread
Still in their places
They are growing
To bless a careful
Searching eye

I wonder once again
If life is speaking
From the grass
For each life has its
Lovely moments
Like white blossoms
Arising
Now and then

My daily walk remains
As life unfolds
In light and shadow
With tomorrow
Bringing
Another surprise

FINDING BEAUTY

In the beholder's eye
Beauty may be found
A judgment
Where each is expert
Whatever others may decide
For in such matters
Each has a say

Yet
Something more
Must still be said
When many agree
Who having been exposed to
Many moments
Whose sense of sight or sound
Or taste align
Whose sensitivities of heart or mind
Resonate
To declare
Now that
Is truly beautiful
So it seems
Experts are born

Yet surely
Each is after all
His or her own expert
With authority for one's self
Such matters to decide
For me
That is really beautiful

IS

I was ambling
For exercise I suppose
When
Pausing at the corner
Where snow white roses grow
Smiling at the day
I stopped
Where a cluster
Of white blossoms
Spoke
Without a word
In inarticulate wisdom
Of profound
Silence

Gazing into a rose's lovely face
I knew
What I could never say
Or could be said
The snowy blossom was in truth
A part of me
As I the rose
Yet
Neither one the other
Though both together
A part of one
Infinite
Reality
In which earth and sky
With all that
In them lies

I stood still
As boundaries faded
Bush and blossoms
Drifting clouds and arching sky
My beating heart
All united in one
Unspeakable
Reality
Together with all
That anywhere may be
Beyond all words
Or singular distinctions
All part of something
That simply
Is

LEAVES

I stroll a path each day
Shaded by
Great shaggy trees
Whose branches filter
Golden sunlight
Casting lovely patterns
Where I walk

Scattered are
Many leaves
Having lost their hold
On a branch that
Gave them birth
Now rest in many
Patterns
Along the way I take

So my life too appears
Born
From a family tree
Whose roots go deep
Into the fertile soil
Of many generations
Each flourishing
In seasons of their time

So my mortal leaf
Gaining nurture from
Its branch
Returns as much virtue
As its limits allow
Until
As for all
Earth's Autumn comes
Then shall I join
The pattern of the years

OF BEES AND BUTTERFLIES

One might say
They're just bugs with wings
Seeking a tasty sip
From the garden's
Grandiose display
Differing in myriad ways
Still sharing
An aerial approach

So do we
In life's more
Complex dimensions
Display
By countless ways
Our search for sustenance
Or satisfaction

The honeybee has tiny wings
That whir to whisk their host
From bloom to bloom
So the butterfly displays
Its flight in lovely
Color and dimension
With a more leisurely approach

So often
We
Like the honeybee
Busy ourselves
Buzzing through our days
From this to that
In what may be
Our own style
Of locomotion

Yet the bee
With daily diligence
Adds to life its sweetness
In the end
While the gentle butterfly
Adds its lovely beauty
To the world
In its brief passing

So are all God's creatures
Made with differences
Their life to live
A gift to give
To the beauty
Of the whole

PERCHED

I perch
Like a bird
Pausing from its flight
Waiting
With cocked ear and eye
To see which way
'Tis best to fly

Large clouds
Dark with rain and thunder
Ride the wind that
Sways this bough
Where now I perch
Waiting for a sign
Which way 'tis best
And when
To fly

REBORN AMONG THE ROSES

It was a grey day
Inside and out
I'd known brighter hours
The fate of all our kind

Unburdened
By any obligation
I ambled down
A shaded path
To an open garden gate
And
Ventured in

I was greeted by a vision
Of breathtaking beauty such as
I had never seen
As a multitude of roses smiled
With lovely faces
Nodding a greeting in a
Gentle breath of breeze
While in that sacred moment
A near transcendent light
Illumined a near-divine display

Along the path
Violet, fuchsia, crimson, gold
Countless forms and faces
Smiled up at me
A wondrous gathering where
Each might be

The work of an angel
Sitting in a quiet nook of Paradise
Carefully shaping Heaven's love
Into a flower

So was I enfolded
Senses born anew
In a dawn of new delight
The air once hard and cold
Now soft
Warm
Caressing

So was a grey and gloomy day
Transformed
The gift of a lovely garden
And sacred beauty of
Flowers

SKY SONG

The soft blue sky
Breathes cloud ships
Gracefully along
Toward far mountain rim
Without a whim
Another day
May change its breath

Yet
Mortal minds recall
Darkened skies
Bearing swirling billows
Of raging aerial hosts
Thunder throated
Lightning laced
Savaging the earth below
With screeching winds
Pelting rain and snow
Until
Blue skies
Breathed 'round again

I muse in my mere
Mortal mind
That
Good weather days
With years of life
Are a treasure
While
The sky reminds
Life's storms will sometime
Have their day

Nonetheless
It's surely best
To celebrate the good
We're given
The sun-splashed days
Heaven's gift
Our gratitude we owe
For life
Open to
The ever-changing drama
Of the years

THE AVENUE OF THE ANTS

On my daily stroll
Along the walk
Cane in hand
Watching where I placed
My step
I saw them
An avenue of tiny ants
Hurrying across my path

It looked like
A frantic
But purposeful procession
Each tiny creature scurrying
Some in one direction
Others headlong in the other
Sharing the same
Invisible avenue
Each seemed to know

I paused to ponder
A lesson from
The sidewalk and
Busy ants
So easily stepped over or upon
By our far larger kind
For we are busy
Hurrying too
Some in one direction
Others
Along avenues of habit
Or necessity
Wondering where our own
Scurrying will end

The ants in their tiny avenue
Often meet head to head
And for an instant
Pause
Their tiny feelers touching
Before scurrying on
Not needing
Conflict resolution

I know my world
As everyone's
Differs in a million ways
Our many sidewalks complex
While we often move
In conflicting directions
Our encounters
Lasting a moment
Or
A lifetime

Yet we may learn
To use our human practice
Of wise compassion
With mutual respect
Clearing life's avenues
For others and ourselves
As we hasten toward
Our divine and
Mutual
Destination

WONDER

God forbid the day should come
Without a pause to
Wonder
A time amid the rush of things
It seems that I must do
To ask if this or that
Could or should be
And if so
Add to the beauty
Of this day or
Others yet to come

Tomorrow holds its mysteries
That time may yet unfold
Although today holds quite enough
To cause a curious mind
To pause and wonder

Is there a message in the soft
Drifting billows of the sky
The flowering garden speaks
Of more than loveliness
As ancient mountains
And high soaring eagle
Join in a silent symphony that
Sounds in a quiet and
Listening heart

So may this day wrap a
Thoughtful soul in rapture
A gift and benediction
The true delight
Of
Wonder

Section II
Pondering

A MATTER OF CONSCIENCE

Right
Or
Wrong
Who's to say
About the many truths
Some definitely declare
One way
Or
The other

When questions come
With decisions on the line
Within us all
Speaks a voice
Calling attention
To what
We have been
Taught to call
Right or wrong
Good or bad
Or even
Something in between

So many voices eager
To decide
Who's to say
Good or bad
Surely it's a matter
Of Integrity

Confidence with either
Brings responsibility
To weigh
Each choice
Pro or con
That inner counsel
Some call conscience
Others call God

Either way
Options stand as
Open doors
Or closed
Depending on
Freedom given
Whatever is decided
Our tomorrows
Await the choice

Thus
Integrity demands
A deciding soul
Must listen
To such wisdom
As years bestow
Lighted by
A well schooled conscience
And
God

AN OPEN DOOR

There it stood
Our front door
Open
Did I leave it ajar
Or did she?
To admit fresh breeze
Or forgotten passing through
Yet
It stood
Welcoming friend or foe
Who knew?

It brought another door to mind
Through it I view
The world
And all of humankind

For all that I might learn or
Virtue would possess
Must pass through
An open mind and heart
The wider world to bless

While I may rise to
Close the door
To keep the breeze or
Unknown others out
To close my mind
Or seal my heart

Would soon betray
My only hope
Learning what
This life's about

Doors are made for
Passing through
According to occasion
But minds and hearts
Open must remain
Welcoming all that enters
For thoughtful
Consideration

Thus I shall rise
As breezes wane
Closing our front door
To return and read a book
With open mind and
Grateful heart
There is always
So much more
To learn

.

CONTEMPLATION

That may be so
But let's give it thought
We've sometimes heard it said
As though
By a bit of careful
Contemplation
A new light may dawn
Revealing a new or hidden truth
Leading to another point of view

Still while this is
Or ought to be
Many times advised
It may clearly be applied
To both sides
Of any argument
Or indeed
Significant discussion

For it is surely clear
An abundance of views abound
Concerning all that matters
As with much that
Just as clearly
Does not

Yet all the same
Clarity and truth are surely
Most likely to be found
At the other end
Of a bit of careful
Thoughtful
Contemplation

DAD'S LOVING TOUCH

Snicklefritz is not my name
But I heard it when
Father mussed my hair
With grinning
laughing eyes
Deciding this playful tag
suited the moment best

Names usually are by
family or nation given
Though now and then friends
may bestow one to reflect
Nature's gift or moment's mood
"Hi, Red"
"Smile, Pickle Puss"

My dad had more in store
I need not mention
Though " Skizzerwinkus" may
take the cake
Given with love
and good intention

Titles awarded in formal settings
are enjoyed when given
Still most are earned
each day in the simple act
of living

Now this long
remembering bard
Still recalls with deep affection
Dad's loving touch
his playful
"Snicklefritz"
or even
"Skizzerwinkus"

DECIDING

Questions always questions
Life is well supplied
Often in matters plain and simple
Such as butter for your
Morning toast
While others clearly bring more
To ponder
Such as issues on the ballot
Which if chosen may impact
Your life the most

Research is called for
On matters of great import
While input from your sense
Of taste
May settle the present matter
Or others of the sort

But the simple truth is
Made plain for us each day
That we really can't escape Deciding
On things what matters greatly
That we face at work
Or at play

For living needs to be supplied
With input from all sides
And we must decide
Which choices made
Will most enhance the life
We dare to dream
Or give our hesitating spirit
Wings

For destiny is a jigsaw puzzle
Its many pieces life-supplied
Our choices will at last disclose
How wise was our deciding
In our time from
What destiny assembled
For our tomorrows

DIFFERENT

With lifted brow and
Widened eye
We heard what
We thought we knew
Until
Something new was said
Another point of view
Was read

How can we know
All that in
Another dwells
For we must sometimes accept
What appears at odds with what
We thought we knew about
Another's thoughts

Until at last we realize
Decisions are often made and
Values grow
From experience we've not shared
But from points of view
With values of their own

Yet
Much indeed is shared as
History and many books
Open for us
Understanding
That is tragic to ignore

So must we understand
That each life has
A pathway of its own
Uniqueness that is
Its treasure
A gift to those who
With lifted brow and
Widened eye
Might someday say
"That is
Different"

GOOD TASTE

Sometimes a matter of
The mouth
At other times a matter of
The mind
In whichever it is found
Good taste is a gift
Of a very special kind

While not a moral virtue
I suppose
For a rascal may admire
Picasso or Van Gogh
While a saint may choose
Cartooning in the morning Post
Though why
Nobody knows

Yet taste in mouth or mind
May surely add a new dimension
A certain flair or flavor
To the day

A striking tie or
Smart new dress
May not make the meal
But buttered pancakes and
Good hot coffee
May make a mighty difference
How you feel

Now it must surely be confessed
The judgment of the masses
Provides a certain kind of test
Some things are said to be so-so
While others of a similar sort are
Thought to be the best

Yet for me
And perhaps for you
We are glad
Whatever critics may decide
To have the freedom
To exercise whatever taste we have
And say
Isn't that just beautiful
And it tastes good too

I'VE OFTEN WONDERED

I've often wondered about
The shape
This old world is in
Though
Others wonder too
Far better qualified than I
To assess the state of things
That compose this troubled
And confusing scene
And why

Environment is out of hand
And rightly a concern
As heat and storms
Devastate far beyond
Historic norms

All the while great nations rage
Threaten heavy sanctions
Now and then
Resort to what are clearly
Devastating actions

Thus I cannot help but face
The question rising in my heart
As I survey the news
Telling in all too grim detail
Of thousands dying
In ongoing wars
While countless others starve
Dreaming of a crust of bread

Is this but tragic repetition
Of what has always been
But will give way
To better years ahead?

Or is it now
As we've been warned
By those prepared to know
Time for all of us to
Face surrender
Of much we treasure most
To stem the tragic tide
That threatens all the earth

IMAGINATION

Pictures in the mind
Some unbidden
Vagabond
To reason or
Reality
Mirroring our memories
Adding fact or fiction to
The drama of the dreams
We call
Imagination

Creative possibility abounds
In that inner world
Where dreams occupy what
Might have been or
Might be
If only
This or that
Should become
Real

Yet that inner world is
Often full
Of color
Life
Song
Beautiful make-believe
Painting a portrait of the
Spirit's passions
Innocent or not

Played out in
The gift
Of the unbound
Imagination

Yet the gift
From rich thoughts
With responsible expression
Brings practical invention
The world moves on
In countless ways
Into a tomorrow
Where all may dream
In the remarkable gift
Of imagination

IN A WORD

You have my word for it
He said
With listeners
Satisfied
Here was one with
Renowned
Integrity

Multitudes would aspire
Such virtue
To attain
Avoid
Misinformation
Forsake
Mistakes
Though infallibility lies
Beyond
All human grasp

Thus
Humility is best
When sharing information
Or opinion
Difference noted
Readily confessed
In respectful conversation

For such may add
To shared perception
That here is one
With true
Integrity

INCARNATION

Sometimes I wonder
Where God is
Given that the world
Seems quite rudderless
And yet
Goes blazing on
Full speed ahead
To wherever we are going
Though who knows to where
And when?

Yes, I'm quite sure
Omnipotence is not asleep
That Deity is not dozing
But has an almighty hand
Upon the switch of fate
But
If that is so
Why then the mess
This world is in of late?

Still
I must admit
It may indeed be me
That has somehow
Misplaced God
And thus wrongly read
Reality

For Jesus, Paul and
All the rest
Each sought to make it plain
That God the Spirit seeks a home
In every human heart
There to be Incarnate
And to reign

Thus in holy wisdom
Guide and steer and thus
Transform this world God loves
Into a place they called
The Kingdom

So if indeed
That is where God lives
Incarnate in fragile souls
Like yours and mine
And all our earth born kind
It must then appear
Earth's destiny resides
In the God-filled hearts
And busy hands
Of just and truly
Loving minds

LEARNING

Beginning
With a baby's cry
Reaching
Nursing
Growing
Learning daily
Do or
Don't
Yes or no
Someday
Perhaps

School and lessons
Read and write,
Study homework
Multiply divide
Follow rules
Playground games
Win and lose
Savor victory
Taste defeat
Find friends

Graduate into a world
To learn its ways
Seeking an
Open door
Open minds
To accept your contribution
Fruit of lessons learned
Thus far

Romance and family
New vocabulary
Calendar altered
Many years ahead
Rich with blessing

Thus flow the years
As does the world
Forever change
Crying babies grow
New lessons learned
As old ways pass

Yet
Each age has taught
To underscore
A truth
That does not change

Life is ever best where
Hearts are warm and kind
Minds compassionate and
Just
And earthly life has learned
To live
In love

MAGNIFICENT

Today I walked
Or
Ambled
Along a path
My present
Years require
Passing through
A garden
Splendidly alive
In spring's full bloom
A glory of fragrant roses

Overflowing
Delicate pink
With deepest crimson
Close beside
Billowing cloud
Of snow white
Gentle lavender
Bloomed beside the
Garden walk
While brilliant yellow
Shading to gold
Entwined the gateway's
Graceful arch

Here I stood
Enthralled
By spring's grand display
Assorted blooms
Of every shape
Every color
A grand montage
Scenting the springtime air
With what must be
Heaven's own perfume

I paused
And smiled
At God
Breathed deep
While a grateful heart
Found a prayer
With
A single word
Magnificent

PONDERING

(with apology to John Calvin)

Deep in thought today
I wonder
About so many things

When and where did
Life begin
And whence the journey's
Ending
Will we find
Joys or sorrows on
The path
The answer comes
Depending

Does Omnipotence decide for all
Is destiny a given
Or depending on the journey
We pursue
Do we create a hell
Or Heaven

Today I contemplate
What pathway I will wander
For tomorrow's journey waits
Beyond the hour
While I pause to
Ponder

REMEMBER

Was it yesterday
Yesteryear
Or the day before
Things we ponder
Our busy minds recall
Pictures of our passing life
Pasted in the
Scrapbook of the mind
Labeled
Memories

Treasures of our years
Remind us
Who we are
Or were
Or might have been
Every recollection
Bringing
A smile
A tear
Birthing for a moment
A yesterday

Still
Forgetting has its place
Where memory may bring
A pain too deep
A shadow on the soul
That only the light of love
May banish
Compassion dissolve
Mercy heal

Remembering
Makes us whole
Learning from our
Yesterdays
Opening pathways
To whatever may be
Our tomorrows light
The lamps of former years
Remembered
As new lamps are lit
The doorway to tomorrow
Opens

STARS IN THE CARPET

Lovely indeed
Dove grey cashmere sweater
Dusted with clouds of
Tiny sequins
Hardly seen
Until she moves

But now and then
One escapes its favored place
Finding a new home
Within the bedroom carpet
Quite unseen until
A ray of light
Discovers for a moment
A tiny glowing face
Within Its secret dwelling place
Until I move
Then
It's gone

So now
I've found my dwelling
In humanity's wide span
Which carpets earth
From pole to pole
Over city, mountain, field or sea
While in such a scene
I remain
Invisible

Yet I hope to find
From fate's kind hand
An illuminating beam
To set my mundane life aglow
With shining face
The sequin in its place

Though now
I realize
The illuminating light
I seek
Awaits within
For me to share with this
Ever-moving world

STILLNESS

Hush
Be still
So many thoughts
Tumble about
Entangle
To make sense of
This or that
Or
Anything at all

Find a time
The wise among us say
To set aside the
Turmoil of the moment
Or the hour
The clamor of the cause
However grand
Then

Breathe deep
Throw open
The mind's windows
To a clear blue inward sky
Free from thoughts
Of anything at all
Until

Quietly as
A drifting cloud
The way you seek
A better path
May come to view

Now
Those wise among us
Who see the good of all
Will counsel

Rise up
And do
With zeal and passion
All
That
Must be done

THE WISH

Wishing will make it so
Declare the lyrics
Sung by all of us who
May also say
If only it were true
Which depends of course
On what you have in mind

If wishing brings to view
A benefit for others
Than just me
A consequence
To make this world a
Better place
It's surely a wish worth having
If it leads to something
We can do

Wishes are but waking dreams
That commoners and holy men
May share
For Jesus it was
The Kingdom coming
That set his disciples dreaming
Though they didn't see a cross
At all

Still a promise their Lord gave them
All they prayed for
Would be given
If in his name and spirit asked
Stones into bread
Mountains into the sea
So John wrote that Jesus said
Though we may think these words
Hyperbole

All have dreams or
Have a wish
Maybe two or three
Bringing color to the day
While also
Birthing plans
For what we hope
Yet may be
Provided
To guarantee
The needed work
Be
Done

THOUGHTS

Life
It just is
That's all
Tho' sometimes not
For all things have
Their end
And yet
Life
A gift
Sometimes goes sour
For many reasons
Complicated
Or not
And crying for an end
Won't help
As much as a
Helping hand
Or loving touch

Life
Sometimes full of
Lovely things
Beauty
Or passion
Brim with meanings
Too plentiful to list
And somehow
In its midst
One may sometimes see
The face of God

WORDS

This world is full of words
With surely no shortage
Really quite enough
As many a word-weary soul
Might say
Though we must further note
It is not their number
But more
Their meaning
That signals significance in
Any collection or expression
Written
Or spoken

For an author uses words
As a painter uses brush
Dipping into his vocabulary
Of colorful expression
Painting a picture to
Touch a lover's heart
Inform a searching mind
Convey understanding to
Set a civic-minded soul aflame

Words
Butterflies in life's verbal garden
Where blooms of every kind
Scent the air with fragrance of
Many meanings
Some, dark foreboding
Others, bright hope

Words
Each glimpse a vision
A doorway to tomorrow
Promising that
Life's final truth shall be
As the ancient text proclaims
The Creator
Declared it
Good

Section III
Along the Way

A MATTER OF TASTE

I licked my spoon
Smacked my lips
My mother's brow gently shadowed
In a frown
Oh but I liked it
I truly did
I said

But what you tasted was not
What I was noticing
Was her motherly reply
Your manner of your tasting
Raised the matter of
A different sort of taste

Many matters
The word taste describes
How we dress
Landscape the yard
Arrange the house
Buy a car and
I suppose
Select a spouse

Taste speaks different words
To describe a way of life
The preferences we choose
Within the possibilities
That circumstance allows
Inherited from family
Culture and society
Until noticed
By other eyes
Hopefully and kindly
By a friend

CALL IT HABIT

It's the way I go
That's all
A touch here
Another there
A door knob
That old chair
Each in the place where
Always found
Except
When someone moves them
Elsewhere
Confusing
My accustomed path

Call it habit
Or another name
It's all the same
Following the
Familiar
Marking my daily path
The furniture of life
All in its place
Silently signaling
The way
It was yesterday and
Days before

Yet
I shall rise
To follow
My accustomed path
To whatever duty
Desire
Or necessity decree
Still hopeful that
Today
I may discover
A path
Beyond
Old habit

For one may
Trust
A kindly Providence
Today
May move the
Furniture of life
Beyond all
Expectation

LIFE SINGS

A newborn baby cries
A song of its beginning
To tell the world
"I'm here"
The first note
Of many
This life
Like every life
Will sing
With many notes and chords

For songs are sung
By raptured hearts
Or exulting minds
In many moods or manners
When no sound
No vocal note is heard

Life's a serenade in
Many harmonies
Melodies in sight or sound
Heard as a symphony
With violins and blaring horns
Timpani or brass

Yet does a garden orchestrate
A vibrant concert
Of its own
Harmonies that trumpet
In bold crimson roses
Or soft yellow daisies
Surrounded
By gentle pianissimo
Of leafy ferns and
Tiny violets

So does a garden sound
A silent serenade
Joining countless ways
Life orchestrates melody
Song
All life together sings

NOW WHERE...

Now where did I...
Could have put
Anywhere
Always
Same place
But now it's not
Probably show up
Sometime
But...

Just my luck
Wouldn't ya' know
Always happens
Appointments galore
Doctor
Bank
Car wash
Trader Joe's
But right now I need
Now where in...
Damn!

What
You did?
But so help me
I looked
Plain sight you say
Wouldn't ya know
Always happens
Anyway
Thanks

Now where did I...

OH NUTS

With dignity I have
No fuss
It cloaks humanity with
Solemn grace
Though sometimes
As indeed these days may be
Grace rebels and
Solemnity retires
So that I would rather
Cuss

Although
Community requires people
To agree on decisions
Often hammered out
In hours or days or more
Of calamitous debate

Yet
Sometimes
A rowdy raucous din
Obscures the better path
And dims the hope
Of any happy ending

So I do confess
In such a time
I defy decorum
Dignity or grace
To inwardly
Or outwardly exclaim
Oh nuts!

ON MESSING UP

Why I didn't do it
I don't know
It seemed straightforward
At the time
Something quite simple to complete
Was I somewhere dreaming
Or just too slow

So I messed up
As the saying goes
And left undone
Or only unsaid
What clearly was my
Social obligation
As everybody knows

Not that my record shows
Unmarred perfection
For like most folks I've
Messed up
In this
Or in some other
Preferred direction

So it's clear that now
As then
I must implore
That Mercy show a kindly face
To this imperfect Pilgrim
Of The Way
And bestow again Heaven's
Undeserved
Redeeming
Grace

PASSING HOURS

The hours pass
Sometimes slowly
It seems
While at others
All too fast
Without our really knowing why

Until suddenly
Tomorrow dawns
And we are prone to wonder
How much of life we've missed
Or has simply
Passed us by

We fill our days
As best we can
And use what gifts
We have been given
Trusting we may finally leave
This world
Some worthy token
Of our swiftly passing years
On our way to Heaven

But all the same
We sometimes pause to wonder
If between our
Now and then
Our hours of
Work or
Dreaming
Rest or playing
Will somehow shape
Our Everlasting Yonder

Yet slow or fast
The hours
The days
The years shall pass
And we must fill them with
Our best
So when our times on earth
Are done
We may rest
Content
At last

PICTURES ON THE WALL

There they are
Pictures on the wall
Placed some time ago
Which now
We pass
Scarcely seeing
What once grasped our attention
And appreciation
Earned their place upon the wall
Where now we pass by
Hardly seeing

But now I pause
Contemplate
Stepping in
Where in my mind
I once desired to be
Breath the air
Catch the breath
Another place
Some other time

Renew an old acquaintance
In a once familiar place
Which now
Only a picture on the wall
For this thoughtful moment
Returns again
To me

Pictures on the wall
Windows to the mind
Remembering
Gateways where the heart may
Enter in
Savoring a passing
Moment
Or perhaps
Longer contemplation
Opening to a time that
Once was
Or might have been
In that moment
Now
Lives again

POLITICS

Politics
Nice or sometimes nasty
Does it have a
Definition
Beyond the name

Since it has been called
The science of government
One might then suppose
It to be
The way we mortals
Get along
In spite of varied temper
And experience

Or perhaps it may be
The system society devises
To define the way
Its common life shall flow
Decisions reached
Responsibilities assigned
To keep both business
And the common life
Most conveniently
And happily
Arranged

But at the heart it seems
Underlying all else that
Might be said
There must be in all of us
A heart that thirsts for justice
Born of love
For all the human race

Definitions come and
Definitions go
But all humankind must learn
To live in ways agreed upon
By those both great and small
To live together
On this amazing earth
In peace, justice
And harmony
So our common life
Shall be
A blessing and a happiness
For all

SHOULDA...

I suppose I really
Shoulda
Since I really
Coulda
If I
Woulda
Though must confess
I didn't

Life's road is filled
With obstacles a-plenty
So we must be wary
In looking back
Without regret
We need not say
"I'm sorry 'cause
I shoulda"

Yet comes the day
When needing to decide
All options appear
Scary
So choosing
May suggest it's time
To be wise and
Wary

Yet come what will
As something must
Tomorrow may reveal
Choices today were best
Because we did
The best we knew
As we
Shoulda

SO GOL-DARN GOOD

There's folks I know
So gol-darn good
I don't know what to call 'em
'caus Saints are s'posed
To look
All Holy like
So's a halo fits 'em

But there's good folk
What don't have frills
Tho they's decent
An' good lookin'
They'll get to heaven
Quick as me
Up where they say
St. Peter does the bookin'

When it comes to kindness
Our friend Nancy is
A mighty thoughtful
Neighbor
Bringin' ice cream
An' good stuff
Right up to our front door

When day's all done
An' darkness falls
She always says goodnight
With a blink or two
From the window sill
With her
Little candle light

TEMPTATION BY TEXT

Lifetime prize
You deserve it
So they say
Response required
Act now

Others in your area
Have
Won before
Now
The drawing just weeks away
Don't neglect to enter
As some have done
A fortune lost

Act now
Place your order
Many special deals
Bargain prices
Customer favorites
Galore
Wow

The enclosed number
Is yours alone
Unless you refuse
Then another will receive it
One who may live nearby
Your fortune might win
With that big bonus as well
Oh my

You're at the very top
The President's Elite
Among those whose
Number will win
Just one more step
So send your entry-order
Now

So reads the text from
*PCH
Week after week
Monthly
Yearly
I don't answer anymore

I must admit
I've purchased a thing or two
Pleased with what's arrived
Pursuing that most elusive purse

Though temptation can be a curse
To resist
I finally understand
All that fills my life
Today
Is treasure enough

*(PCH=Publishers Clearing House)

THE PATH

Natal day
A journey
Begins
A pathway through
Unknown tomorrows
Planned
Or dreamed
By those ardently caring
Unfolding through days
Years
Filled with sun or rain
Joy and laughter
Sometimes
Tears

Onward the pathway leads
Through quiet meadows
Verdant green
Where flowers bloom
Leafy trees shade
A weary traveler
While beyond
Unseen may rise
A forbidding forest
Dark with question
Shadowing the rock-strewn path
To suddenly reveal
The face
Of an ominous wall

Yet
The trail ascends
To an unknown summit
Where
Beyond
Life's varied journey
Moves on to
A descending path
Where challenges continue
But joys remain
An adventure
Deepened
By gratitude

Surely we must
Remember
Trust
While caring
Loving
Arms embrace
The world

Until at last
Evening brings
An ending
Though
Faith may view
Beyond

THERE ARE TIMES

There are indeed those times
When what has always seemed
So clear
That I took it quite
For granted
Has at this moment
Become a bit
Opaque

Which means I suppose
That in my mind
And heart
I do wonder
Even as I know
The Hand that holds me will
Never let us part

Still
In this blessed bondage
I am free
To question and to wonder
Even as life brings its
Quandaries to the fore

For I know quite well
The answers that I seek today
May lie
Well beyond my mortal ken
And yet
In faith I trust that
When my days on earth are done
I shall learn the answers to all
That seemed opaque in those times
Back then

THOUGHTS IN PASSING

Here I sit and ponder
Letting random thoughts just
Come and go
Nowhere I suppose
But then
Who knows

Sometimes I wonder
Now and then
About tomorrows on the
Calendar and those beyond
Where the tides of time
May take us
And to what end

Of course the future
Is opaque
In spite of studied
Calculation
Of Dow Jones averages
With how the market fares
And more
Or even what the preacher
On the corner says
Though he quite clearly
Doesn't know
The score

But thoughts do wander back
To glean what wisdom
Or comfort may be found
From days or years gone by
And even wish sometimes
We could turn
Father Time
Around

But as we wander
In mind's eye
Through tomorrow's
Busy streets
Or climb the future's
Daunting hill
We best remember
That whatever
Lies beyond tomorrow
Will find us still
As always
In the timeless care of
Eternal Love

TO BE WISE

Surely it is wisest
To know and then choose well
Understanding that the
Choices made today
May well define the way ahead
Thus to select the path that
Promises the happiest tomorrow
Appears to be
Wisdom

Yet
More is required than
Accumulated knowledge
Of many assorted facts
For true wisdom is much more
Than this
Rather it is born in knowing
How life's pieces best assemble
Guided by
Perception and perspective
Of one's own experience born
Yet in no small measure
From studying what the wisest
In their time discerned

So does wisdom come in gathering
Life's data and its
Often confusing facts
Sifting and selecting
What exposure and the
Council of the ages may suggest

Then with humility assembling
Our own point of view
A worthy, workable perspective
To choose the path
Where life's enduring values
Are practiced
And protected
So that
Wisdom guiding
All our world
Is blest

VIRTUE

A standard there must be
Before virtue claimed
Or perhaps assigned
For better
Best
Or in between
When judged by comparison with
A scale most widely held
By those for whom such
Things matter

But whence the standard
For there is not merely one
But many
Formed by those sharing life
Together
In their own unique tribe or
Neighborhood
City
Town or state

Still
Within them all in
Large or small degree
There runs a golden thread in the
Loom of common days
Weaving a pattern
Creating a fabric of many standards
Ways of life
Guiding all who would part of
The pattern be

Not all weave well
Tangling and breaking the thread
Tearing the fabric
Betraying those who strive
To weave a better world

Yet for all who
Seek to live and play their part
In weaving together
A world of
Justice and
Love for all
A claim to virtue in
Large or small degree
Is theirs to rightly claim
Though by others
Best bestowed

WHILE THE SUN SHINES

I sit beside the window
Behold this sunlit day
Trees grass and
Garden's beauteous flowers
Each splashed
With golden sun

With it comes
Calm reflection
That life itself is much the same
With hours and days and years
That bless the soul in passing
Sunny days that
Overflow the heart
With gratitude
Even while
Quietly remembering
Twilight will sooner fall
Until at last
Night will come
Wrapping all within
Its sable arms

So it is clearly wise
To rise
And venture into the sun
Heart wide open
To the beauty of this day
Finding there some way
That life yet may be
A gift

To give some shadowed soul
A splash of joy
A touch of Heaven's love
While daylight lasts

So when my day is done
And nighttime falls
Wrapping all my world
In gentle sleep
I shall be glad
I rose up

Section IV
Nearing the Top... and Over

A PRAYER AT EVENTIDE

As slows the day
And twilight softens
And restfulness comes on
Dear God of each day's length
Who sees the end
From the beginning
I turn again to thy dear arms
While my ever trusting soul
Awaits thy bidding
For the swiftly passing years
Have been rich with blessing
And my heart
Is full and overflowing
With the goodness of my God
And so
Dear Father
At life's eventide
I lay me down to rest
Perhaps to wake
Beyond the silver morning
Home at last
In that long awaited place
Where all is loveliness
And Peace
And earth's eventide gives way
To Heaven's greater dawn

A SENSITIVE MATTER

It is often said to be a matter
Forbidden to discuss
Unless
You are speaking with a friend
Who views the world
Much the same
As you
Give or take
A Senate bill
Or two

And of course
Religion is included in the ban
So it's a wise suggestion
To save your
Sacred conversation
To share with those whose
Data on the Deity
Has more in common with
Your own

But if perchance you stumble
Into a forbidden conversation
The time quite ripe may be
To share the light
That you've been given
And perchance receive an
Unexpected revelation

For wisdom comes to those
Who know that those who most
Politic would be
Are those who gladly share
A humble and an open mind
With friend and foe alike
Knowing that
True wisdom is the friend
Of those who meet the world with a
Just and loving
A truly human heart

AS TIME MOVES ON

So time moves on
To what or where
Or even when
One might inquire
Tho' the answer
Eludes our mortal mind
Still the answer does remain
To give pause
When
As all life must
We find we are growing old

The evidence is really not
A calendar affair
Nor do mathematics
Shed much light
Or genetics
Much inform

Rather it seems
The evidence is on display
In graying hair
And wobbly knees
And no doubt
Another ache or two

Yet all the same
It would surely be amiss
Not to count the many gifts
These added years bestow

The long perspective
And the plus of patient wisdom
The treasure of abundant blessing
Scarce counted in the
Frantic rush of youthful days
Now added to a
Quiet gratitude to God
And the peace old age may add
That passes youthful understanding

DAYBREAK

Gone
My beloved friend
Is dead

Oh he knew
Sooner or later for us all
Heaven awaits
He's Home at last
Pearly gates swung wide

But will we see pearly gates
Mansions tall
Golden streets
Winged angels praising God
Upon His throne
As ancient fantasy proclaims?

So I once believed
When I gave my heart to Jesus
Where it remains today
Yet passing years
Of life's adventure
The works of studied minds
Have shed a clearer light
For me

Still Jesus' love reminds me
Many faithful follow paths
Unlike my own
Legends of shining Heaven
Welcome by the Kingly Christ
Remain the heart of Assurance

Firm and blest
For them

As for him we've lost awhile
Time to depart has arrived
A shining Heaven waits

While at those pearly gates
Long lost loved ones stand
Arms spread wide
Welcoming their beloved
Home

Still for those
Who see another light
In studied history
A sacred story shines anew
Where Jesus walks with dusty feet
Through Galilee
To teach
To bless and heal
The common folk
Who were
His own

Full of the Spirit
Of love and justice
That is God
With passion for a Kingdom
Now
And yet to be
He lived
And died
And lives
Forever

For those who well know
The ancient tales
Yes, for all
Passing from this life
Remains a mystery
While one conviction holds fast
Welcome by a loving God
And glorious
Daybreak

ENDING

To all things comes
An ending
For ancient mountains
The hardest rock
For the gentle butterfly
That flits among the roses
Or the bloom that graces
For a time
The dandelion in the grass

It is quite clear
That those now living
As all else
In time shall crumble and
Have their end

So as I write these lines
It is plain
I cannot exclude myself
Or you
Or anyone at all
Though those rejoicing in their
Fresh humanity
May feel I am rushing it a bit

Not so
Indeed to be aware is
To be grateful
For the adventure and the blessing
Of each day
Be their sum substantial
Or few

For wisdom comes in knowing
Duration is not the key
To virtue or happiness
Either one
For antiquity bears witness
That those who thrived
In happiness or sorrow
Yet left their imprint on the ages
Thought their time was
Brief or long

So may we view our days
Or passing years
Counting not their sum
But treasuring what our labors
May produce
Or happiness supply
Remembering
Our someday ending will grant us
A promised new beginning
Never
Ending

FAITH

I know a place
Where a heart may rest
From those wild winds
That shred life's fragile sail
A place where peace and hope
With promise shine
To light the pilgrim's way
The path by faith in
One who
Has gone
This way before

I have seen storms
Winds and waves
That overwhelm
Fierce tempests
That the Savior knew
Who stayed the course
Until
His journey's end
Bidding all who would follow
To trust his Father's mighty hand
Holding fast to faith that
As for him
A new dawn
Will break
And life begin again

I know a place
Where hearts may rest
A place where faith holds fast
To Him who trusted Almighty Love
Would outlast the fiercest storm
To wrap the world at last
In justice
Love
And
Peace

HOPE

I do hope so
You've often heard
A sentiment so often shared
When the outcome is
Mutually desired
Yet not certain for
Tomorrow
Though perhaps
Sometime

Hope
Seeks an anchor for
The heart
To moor one's dreams
Securely
In days to come
So is
Faith hope's longed-for
Companion
On the journey of our days
Giving hope its bright
Assurance
In the turmoil of
Life's ways

As Hebrews in the wilderness
Or Columbus on a rolling sea
Clung fervently to hope
Almighty Love embraced
Their pilgrim journey
As it does today
For you and me

With hope
Each day our companion
Upheld by faith's
Strong helping hand
We trust the Love
That holds us fast
Will lead us
To our
Promised Land

IMMANENCE

It's almost here
The storm predicted
Is almost here
Immanent they say

The preacher spoke
Of immanence as well
Quoting from
A selected Bible text
Jesus will come again
All signs now align
It could be any day
It's immanent you know

O but he's always coming
As Easter annually declares
Although once crucified
He yet lives
In hearts and minds
Where faith and love like his
Have spread like a holy fire
Around a troubled world

Although the earthly Kingdom
Has not come
As he
And we
Still pray
While many nations choose
A less than just or loving way

His Kingdom on Earth
May only come
When laws and customs
In every life
His loving Spirit dwells

Yet still today
In many a church or mission
A dawn of Jesus's truth and love
Still breaks
As in another life the
Ever living Lord
Will come

MY OLD CHAIR

So here I sit
In my old chair
A gentle breeze
From the ceiling fan
Cools my face

Though the sunlit garden
Just beyond the screened door
Suggests
A lovely day awaits outside
Yet
Here I sit
Contemplating the reasons
Why I am here and not
Out there

Of course my chair
Is quite accustomed
To the oldster I've become
My bumps and bulges
The bony limbs once clothed
With a much more youthful me
And through passing years
Has made gradual adjustments
To my more senior frame

Now
On this most pleasant day
Both in and out of doors
This old chair still serves me very well
So I say
With quiet contented smile
I am truly thankful for you
My old chair

NEVER TOO LATE

The calendar can be a tyrant
If I let it be
As though tomorrow would
Mark the end
Of all the days and times
Allotted me

But of course
That sort of thought has
Crossed my mind before
Although so far
I'm glad to say
Always dawns
One day more

So I
Since given
Providential leisure
I'll pen a word or two
To give someone the pleasure
Of hearing that for them
Yet may be
Many good days more

Today may have its minutes
The calendar its warning
Though it goes to say
Once more
We have time still to do today
What should be done
Before tomorrow morning

RETROSPECTIVE

Thirty years ago you said
I do
When the parson looked to me
I gladly said
Me too
Or words that meant the same
Thus by church and culture blest
Our grand journey
Had begun

Thirty years have passed
So much enjoyed
Adventure filled
As tourists on the go
Traveling the tossing sea
To long dreamed-of lands
Treasures purchased
Here or there
Destined for the coffee table
By the couch at home

So it was
Every passing year was blest
With a multitude of friends
And moments enjoyed
While we seemed
Ever on the run
So this grand adventure
Continued
Touched with love and joy
And fun

Still
As life must be
Arrived some losses too
As time and fate moved on
Beloved family and friends
Many tears were shed

Yet today
Warm sun still shines
While as twilight falls
A gentle moonlight will bathe
A pleasant
Restful night

We will rise at dawn
To live another day
To do what must be done
God given
Until this grand adventure ends
When the next begins
In Heaven together

SEQUESTERED

I could call it
Tucked away
Or even set aside
Though that implies a
Lesser state
Where I would rather
Not reside

Yet times arise
In days like this
When circumstances
Coincide
When things pile up
To demand
A pause
Or maybe a full stop
To let life's pell mell race
Move swiftly on
Without my intervention
However virtuous the cause

Yet today the cause becomes
A must
To bring a deadly virus to an end
To stay at home or
Mask when going out
Becomes consideration
For a friend

So I do not complain
Being tucked away or
Even sequestered
For a spell
Participating in the work
Of healing for us all

For the day will dawn
When we'll fling wide the door
To step unfettered
By this virus or
Anything at all
Rejoicing once again
In freedom's
Blessed light

THE WHEREABOUTS OF GOD

Many are those
Who want to know
The whereabouts of
God
Supposing the Holy One is
Something
Or a someone
Celestial and grand
A divine substantiality
Beyond all human
Contemplation

A cynic might assert
Such a God to be
A divine circusmaster in a
Cosmic ring
Bible in one hand
In the other
A whip

Although in truth
The holy ones of every
Land and time agree
The Sacred One is not
A thing at all
But a Spirit
As near and close to
Everyone and everything
As to the farthest star

Yet these holy ones agree
God is
A Divine Breath
Breathing through every land
Every nation

Thus it appears
That they who seek the
Dwelling place of God
Should undertake
A thoughtful searching
Of the heart
An inventory of the mind
To see if there dwells the Spirit
Of justice and of love
Mercy and compassion
For all of humankind
(The Spirit Jesus knew so well)

This Spirit does embrace
Every one and every thing
And those who such a
Spirit find
Have indeed found at last
The whereabouts
Of God

TRANSCENDENCE

To rise above
All heights
Reached before
To eclipse the
Highest
Greatest
Most profound
Something
Is what every
Striving
Straining
Contemplating
Praying
Pondering
Practicing
Seeker
Tries to attain
Or even
Understand

Yet the answer
May be
Serious as the cosmic quest
Or silly
As
How fast a cat can
Climb a tree

Still transcendence
Matters
When we speak of God
For Divine Reality
Lies beyond
Sight
Sound
Or touch

Love
Justice
Joy
Compassion
Hope and more
In human heart
Are born
Expressing in this
Troubled world
Words or deeds
The Transcendent Spirit
We call
God

TRUST

I raised my eyes
My hopes
My expectations
Though the ceiling remained
Opaque
I knew
Heaven could shine through
And faith might see
Where mortal eyes could not

Then
It came
The voice from deep within
One word
Trust
I knew the tone was mine
Yet I doubted not
That voice belonged to God

So where was God
In some far off Heaven?
Or nearby
In my own heart
Speaking that one word
Trust

I still needed
A missing note
To bolster
My tepid trust
In the one
Who spoke within

I then recalled that John
Once spoke for Jesus saying
He would by his spirit dwell within
One with his Father and
We one with them
To do love's work
On earth

So did I learn
To look beyond all ceilings
To rather
Listen to the One
Who sounds like me
Yet speaks within
To say
On this and all days
Trust

(John 14:18-23)

Final Thoughts

WORDS, WORDS, WORDS

One
Or two
Often many more
Spawned in the brain
That
Gleaned them
From the ear or eye's
Adventure

Words
Sought or simply heard
In living
Bits and pieces
Describing
Defining
To put the world together
Yielding good
Or ill

Words
Painting pictures
A garden's gentle glory
Dawning's bright awakening
Or sunset's blazing farewell
To another day
The wonders of the world

Countless meanings of
A heart's desire
Voicing a mind's profound conviction
To gather the sum of living
With an open mind
A loving heart
All this and more
Words may seek to say

Printed in the United States
by Baker & Taylor Publisher Services